From Herd Boy to University Lecturer

Published by
Mzuni Press
P/Bag 201 Luwinga
Mzuzu 2

Co-published with Luviri Press as *Biographies of People and Parishes* no. 5

ISBN   978-99960-60-70-0
eISBN 978-99960-60-71-7

Mzuni Press is represented outside Malawi by:
African Books Collective Oxford (order@africanbookscollective.com)

www.mzunipress.blogspot.com
www.africanbookscollective.com

Cover and editorial assistance: Daniel Neumann

From Herd Boy to University Lecturer

An Autobiography

Handwell Yotamu Hara

Mzuni Press

Biographies of People and Parishes
no. 5

Mzuzu

2019

Content

Preface

Rev Dr Handwell's book "From Herd Boy to University Lecturer" is very inspiring and worth reading. It describes how God calls a person from humble beginnings and guides to serve Him in various ways. Here is a man God had appointed at a very tender age and who rose to serve in very important positions. Handwell was indeed an ordinary boy from a village in Mzimba. His early life is similar to that of David who was a shepherd but became a very great King in Israel. From illiterate parents Handwell managed to start learning at a village school. He latter attained his highest academic achievement—Doctor of Divinity—at Pretoria University in South Africa. His contributions were numerous. He became a primary school teacher, a lecturer at Zomba Theological College and at Mzuzu University. He also served the church in various positions. He was a congregational minister, became Education Secretary as well as Synod Clerk of CCAP Nkhoma Synod.

As a human being, Dr Hara was not without challenges both at his early age as well as during his service in the church. However, the Lord sustained him and he succeeded. I this respect, the book would have been called "From Herd Boy, University Lecturer to Church Leader."

I therefore implore all to read this book and be inspired.

Winston R. Kawale (Rev Dr)

12 April 2019

Chapter 1: Birth and Boyhood of Handwell Yotamu Hara

Beneka Handwell Yotamu Hara was born on 9 February 1942 to Yotamu Chimodzimodzi family of Jonathan Hara Village, T/A Mwaro in Mzimba district.[1] He was given the name Beneka at birth, a shortened version for Benekelera which means to cover. His father's name was Yotamu Hara and his mother's name was Midani Chaungwe. They were both illiterate, but his mother was a Christian of the Church of Central Africa Presbyterian (CCAP).

Yotamu and Midani had five children namely, Loyiti, Tuwepo, Beneka, Chihambe and Makayiko who died in infancy after Midani's death. When Midani died the baby Makayiko was taken care of by his grandmother Zigatya Ziwa, the mother of Yotamu, but died a few months later due to lack of care.

The four children changed the names they were given at birth. Loyiti changed to Grandson; Tuwepo preferred to be called Dayi-vase; Beneka became Handwell and Chihambe became Christopher. It was a tradition that when children reached a certain age they could either retain their birth names or change to the ones they were happy with.

After the death of Midani, Yotamu married her step sister called Thandiwe Chaungwe. Midani and Thandiwe had the same father, but different mothers. Thandiwe's mother was Nyachisi and Midani's mother was Nyasoko. Their husband was Robert Chaungwe. The philosophy of the elders in advising Yotamu to marry Midani's sister Thandiwe was that she would look after the children Midani had left better than any other woman unrelated to the children. She would not be a stranger to the children who already called her in Chitumbuka *amama achoko*.[2] The case of the

---

[1]   9 February is not the exact date of his birth. He made it up to have a birth celebration. The year is indeed 1942.

[2]   "Amama achoko" means "little mother", my mother's young sister.

children was more valued than the love between Yotamu and Thandiwe.

Thandiwe,[3] however, did not treat the children as Yotamu's advisors had thought she would. She often told Yotamu that the children did not respect her as their step-mother. Although she assumed the role of the mother, she was and remained Thandiwe and she never became Midani. Yotamu scolded the children for not giving her the respect she wanted. The relationship between their father, step-mother and children became sour. Grandson and Dayivase were old enough to see the difference in the treatment given by Midani, their biological mother, and that of Thandiwe, their step-mother. However, the elders still maintained that the relationship between Yotamu and Thandiwe was better than it would have been had Yotamu married a woman from a different family unrelated by blood to the children.

Thandiwe bore Yotamu a baby girl, Ndindase, who was born after Yotamu's death.[4] Yotamu died by committing suicide; he hung himself with a rope in his house. He had sent his wife Thandiwe and his two children—Dayivase and Christopher—to Robert Chaungwe village. Handwell had already been sent to a distant relative called Hayigini Hara. Before Yotamu committed suicide, he went to Bubeni Village to give Handwell an axe to use in his work, for he did not have anything to leave for him. Handwell had gone to look after the flock and although he was told about the axe, he never saw it because the people who received it did not give it to him. Grandson had already left the family to go and live with Rachael Chaungwe at Mponela in Dowa district. The reasons why Yotamu committed suicide were not known, but it was rumoured that he was bewitched by his brother Timeyo Hara

---

[3] Thandiwe means the beloved one.
[4] Ndindase means the stranded one who does not know where to go.

either to hang himself or to throw himself into a river that was full of running water. He hanged himself.

Handwell had attended standard one before he lived with the Hayigini family. He became a herd boy for this family for almost two years. He was paid literally nothing for looking after the flock—cattle, goats and sheep—except receiving nsima,[5] and that only in the evenings. When the cows had their young ones, he prepared "bala la luwisi/phala la mkaka"[6] as his breakfast. He left some for the boys who went to school. The family he lived with were Presbyterian Christians. They used to pray every morning when they woke up, before they ate lunch, and before they went to bed. The boys he was living with cultivated a prayer lifestyle. Handwell learned prayer life while he lived with the Hayiginis.

The five boys slept in their own house called *mphala*.[7] They all went to school except Handwell. These boys were: Dickson and Foster, Hayigini's children; Stocker, Ophaniel Hara's son and Murray, the son of the young brother of Ophaniel and Hayigini. The latter was suspected of practicing witchcraft, a story which Handwell believed to be true. He used to take his children, Dickson and Foster, away from the house at night, through magic, when the rest of the children were asleep. One night, Dickson and Foster woke up Handwell to go out with them to practice witch-craft. But their father, not wanting them to take him, made him go back to sleep and he slept till morning. When he woke up the next morning, he remembered what had happened at night but

---

[5] *Nsima* is a Malawi traditional food cooked as thick as porridge and taken with vegetables, beans or meat.

[6] "Bala la luwisi" (Chitumbuka) /"phala la mkaka" (Chichewa) means milk porridge.

[7] *Mphala* means a small house where boys sleep. It may also mean a place where men eat food together and settle disputes.

could not ask them where they had gone, neither could he tell the incident to anyone.

As a herd boy, Handwell got no pay. Hayigini did not appreciate Handwell's work. He often scolded him for any small mistake he made telling him to go back to his village although at that time his father had already died. One day a cow had given birth and the calf was not strong enough to follow its mother. Since there were a lot of cattle the cow and its calf were left behind without Handwell's knowledge. When he got home the cow was missing and when Hayigini learnt about it, he scolded Handwell, calling him "Chindere Chambulamahara."[8] Hayigini himself used to tend the flock before Handwell joined the family. Early in the morning he went to graze the flock until the children came back from school and took over. Then he could go home, rest a little before doing other work. During the rainy season he worked in his *zingiliza munda*.[9]

Handwell's life during his stay with the Hayigini's family was so bad that he wanted to go back home although his father had died and there was no house to stay in. He could not stay with his nephew in their house. His uncle Timeyo had already separated from his brother Yotamu and their relationship had been bad even before Yotamu died. Handwell was afraid to go and live with his uncle, who was well known for witchcraft practices, but now, living with the Hayigini family, was as bad as being in prison. Eventually, Handwell went to live with his uncle where his sister, Dayivase, was married and his brother Grandson was still at Mponela in Dowa. Handwell's life was now worse than what he had experienced when he was with the Hayigini family.

---

[8] The Chitumbuka phrase means stupid without wisdom.

[9] "Zingiliza munda" means a garden around or near one's house.

Christopher lived with an uncle who had three wives—Nyangala, Nyahojani and Nyaziwa with whom he had several children. Christopher ate the food which the uncle and his elder sons left, called *makombo*.[10] They deliberately left food for the young ones. He ate the food with his younger nephews who, when they had not eaten enough, could go to their mothers for additional food to fill their stomachs. Christopher went to his grandmother, Zigatya, who was often given food by Timeyo's wife. Zigatya always left a small portion of food for him, without which Christopher would have starved. Handwell joined this life when he came back from the Hayigini's family.

Christopher was not taken by his sister, Dayivase, to live with her because traditionally, in those days among the Haras, it was forbidden for a married woman to take her brother to her husband's village. She could only take her sister to live with and serve her. Life for Handwell and Christopher was worse than for of Dayivase and Grandson, but there was no way it could be changed for the better.

As a young boy Handwell could spend most of his day playing with his friends, while the evenings were hard times because he usually slept without eating enough food. When it was time to sleep he had no blanket except a small piece of cloth which he wore during the day. He slept near a coal fire during the cold months of May to July to keep himself warm. He slept on a piece of a reed mat into which he sometimes rolled himself as if he were already dead and ready to be buried.

This was the condition in his boyhood not only after his father's death, but even before his father died. His father was one of the poorest people in the area. It is said that he married one of the most beautiful women of his time. It was also rumoured that

---

[10] "Makombo" is the food the elders leave for the young ones.

Timeyo coveted Yotamu's wife and that he wanted to get her from him. It was believed that because Yotamu's wife, Midani, refused to marry him, she was being bewitched to death.

One unforgettable incident that happened in Handwell's boyhood was that he hurt himself when he hit his cousin on the head with his fist. When they were playing on the sand in Photosa River, his cousin insulted him by calling him a bad name. Instead of calling his cousin a bad name in return, he hit him on the head and it was his fist instead that felt very painful while his cousin laughed at him, feeling no pain. His fist was so painful that Handwell immediately stopped hitting his cousin. From that time Handwell never hit his cousin again fearing that he would hurt himself. He did not follow the "tooth for tooth" retaliation (Exodus 21:38), for if he had followed this method by calling his cousin a bad name in return he would have avoided hurting his fist.

Handwell's father had a short temper; he would easily get angry with little irritations. Both young and old people were afraid of him because once irritated he became angry he would get hold of anything and hit a person with. All of Yotamu's children were afraid of him. People tried all means to help him change his behaviour towards his children, but he did not change. One day he sent Handwell with a chicken to a Mr Nguluwe to breed it for him (*kupazya*) and while he was going, the chicken flew away from his hands and disappeared in the bush. Handwell felt sorry for what had happened and thought that if he reported the matter as it happened, his father would become angry and beat him up.

Instead, Handwell reported that he had given the chicken to Mr Nguluwe. The following day his father went to Mr Nguluwe, who refused having received a chicken from Handwell. Handwell's father was angry with Mr Nguluwe, thinking that he had intended to steal his chicken. People were called to settle the dispute between Yotamu and Nguluwe, with Handwell still insisting that he had given Mr Nguluwe a chicken. Others thought that Handwell might have lost the chicken and was afraid to tell his father the truth. So they postponed the discussion for two days. Before the second day some people saw a chicken in the bush and when they caught it, it was identified to be the chicken Mr Nguluwe was accused of hiding. So the matter was settled and Yotamu did not beat Handwell for what he had done.

The people told Yotamu that it was his cruelty that made his son Handwell to lie, saying that he had given the chicken to Nguluwe when he had not. Handwell lied to his father in order to escape the beating he would get. Fear of his father's reaction made his son fabricate a story which implicated Mr Nguluwe in a theft case.

Before Grandson married, Handwell left the Hayigini family and joined Christopher at his uncle Timeyo's home. Later, Grandson returned from Mponela and joined his brothers. The condition was better than what Handwell had experienced at the Hayigini family. Grandson married, and Handwell and Christopher were put in school. Their uncle Timeyo treated them well because Grandson was old enough and as a married man he needed to be respected. Handwell did well at school and passed standard 3 at Baula. Standard 3 in the 1950s was the class when pupils would write Nyasaland National Government Examination to go to standard 4. Although Handwell had passed standard 4 Grandson could not afford to pay for his fees.

Before he left school Handwell felt being called to the Holy Ministry to be an evangelist or preacher. This happened in July 1958 when he was 16 years old while he was still in standard 3. One afternoon, around three o'clock and during Arithmetic lesson Handwell heard a voice telling him that he would be an Evangelist and a Pastor. He would preach and teach people in different places. The voice did not separate being an Evangelist and being a Pastor and teaching from preaching. He did not share his experience with anyone even when provoked. People thought that he was sick because he remained in that condition of silence for several days. From that time Handwell's behaviour, the way he spoke with others and his dressing changed and became better. He respected other people more than before and he kept himself smart.

Chapter 2: Handwell Leaves for the Central Region

When Grandson could not pay Handwell's fees for standard 4 at Ekwendeni, he put him under Gibson Hara to teach him tailoring work. However, before Handwell became a fully qualified tailor Gibson died of tooth ache at Ekwendeni mission hospital. Thus, Handwell's tailoring course under Gibson ended there. Nonetheless he looked for work as a tailor which he got at Kafukule Trading Centre. After working for a month, he went home to give Grandson his pay to keep for fear it might be stolen. Before he returned to Kafukule his uncle Timeyo invited him for a meal (*nsima*). Although there were four people who ate together from one plate, it was believed that his uncle mysteriously gave him a poisoned piece of food (*thongo*) which did not affect him immediately.

Handwell returned to his work the following day. But before he started work he suffered serious pains in his stomach. He took several pain killer tablets; they did not work. After a week, and still feeling pain, Handwell went back home to seek more help. There was no health centre at Kafukule. The hospitals were far away, one at Ekwendeni and the other one at Mzimba Boma. Although Grandson knew that his uncle Timeyo was accused of practicing witchcraft, he still asked him to prepare medicine for Handwell to cure him of stomach pains. Grandson was also a popular medicine man. The uncle prepared more poisonous medicine for Handwell which, when he took it, made him worse, possibly he wanted to kill him instantly. When Grandson saw that Handwell became worse rather than becoming better, he went to another medicine man, a Mr. Nyirenda, who told him that Handwell was fed poisonous food (*nsima*) by his uncle. The food does not get digested and would eventually kill the boy.

Mr Nyirenda prepared medicine for Handwell to neutralize the poison. The medicine overpowered the poison, the food got digested and Handwell was healed. However, a week later, when Grandson was happy that Handwell was well, he, Handwell, became mentally confused and ran away from home. When Grandson saw that Handwell was mentally confused and had run away from home, he went back to Mr Nyirenda to report what had happened. Mr Nyirenda told Grandson that Handwell had now been cured and the confusion he was experiencing was an indication that the poisoned medicine had lost its power. When uncle Timeyo found out that Handwell was cured, he became angry with Grandson that he had abandoned his medicine without telling him. He thought that Grandson had discovered that Timeyo had fed Handwell poisonous food in order to kill him. The relationship between Timeyo and Grandson broke down.

Grandson now stopped eating food together with his uncle and his cousins. Instead, Grandson ate food only with his two brothers Handwell and Christopher. Although Handwell was cured of the stomach pains and of mental confusion, he did not go back to Kafukule Trading Centre. He was also not well enough to resume his work as a tailor. So he remained at home for several months. When the grandfather, Robert Chaungwe (Midani's father), died, Rachel Chaungwe, his first-born daughter, went from Mponela to Mzimba to her village to attend her father's funeral. She found Handwell recovering from his stomach pains and mental confusion. When she went back to Mponela she took Handwell with her without telling his uncle Timeyo. This is how Handwell came to the Central Region in 1959.

When Handwell arrived at Mponela he looked for work as a tailor but could not find any. It was because he was not fully qualified as a tailor and, in addition, he had just recovered from a mental confusion. He then went to Nkhonde tobacco estate to look for work as a clerk, keeping records of the number of tobacco leaf sticks people produced a day. A tobacco leaf stick had twenty-four tobacco leaves hanging on it and to pluck the required number of tobacco leaves for the day. For one who was quick took six hours.

One would start plucking at 7.30 am and stop at 1.30 pm. He would then go for lunch which was usually thick porridge (*nsima*) with beans. Some slow pluckers went for food at 12 noon and went back to pluck more tobacco leaves in order to finish their required lot of tobacco leaf sticks. Handwell, because he counted the number of tobacco leaf sticks for the pluckers, worked for the whole day from 7.30 am to 12 noon and started again after lunch time which he took either at 12 noon or at 1.30 pm. Tobacco leaf plucking season was a very busy time and required many pluckers, otherwise the leaves would go bad and that would be a great loss. The plucking of the tobacco leaves lasted for two or three months because the tobacco seedlings were transplanted at different times.

After working at the tobacco estate as a clerk for two months, Handwell heard a disembodied voice telling him to resign from his work and prepare for evangelism and preaching work. As he began writing the letter of resignation, a messenger came to call him to the manager's office where he was told that his work was terminated because the tobacco leaf plucking was near the end. Handwell was paid the same day and he went to his aunt at Tembo village. He did not understand what the voice meant because he would not become a pastor or an evangelist for a number of reasons. He was a standard 3 young man and would not go for either an evangelism or a ministerial course; he was not yet baptized as a Christian and he was unmarried.

When Handwell came back from Nkhonde tobacco estate, he did not stay with his aunt to help her with the work at home. His cousins had all grown up. The women were married and lived with their husbands while the men were married and went away to work—some in Lilongwe and others in Blantyre. Handwell decided to go to Lilongwe where he worked for a Mr Mtambo, manager for Costantine Company, as a house boy. Mr Mtambo was married, but he and his wife were on separation and Handwell did not see his wife during the time he worked for Mr Mtambo. Handwell's work involved buying and preparing food; washing Mr Mtambo's clothing; cleaning the house, the utensils and all other items in the house.

Mr Mtambo lived with his nephew who was lame (he had a withered left leg) using a stick to support him in walking. Handwell did most of the work at the house. Handwell lived with Mr Njiko who had married his cousin Yunesi Moyo but was now divorced and Mr Njiko lived alone. Handwell slept in the house of Mr Njiko not very far away from Mr Mtambo's house. He woke up each day at about 4 am. He made fire to warm water for Mr Mtambo and prepared his breakfast before he left for work at 7 am. Handwell had little time to rest even on Saturdays and Sundays, except that on these days he woke up an hour later than usual. He never attended church worship nor went to watch any games. The only time he left the house was when he was sent to buy food items or do other things for his boss. Since Handwell wanted to go back to school to further his education he resigned from his work as a house boy. All this time the voice was silent concerning evangelism and pastoral work.

Instead of going to Tembo village to start school, Handwell went to Dowa to his cousin Crispin Nyirenda, the son of Rachael Chaungwe, who was a brick layer. He found work there as a brick layer assistant. He found the work hard especially in giving bricks to brick layers and taking the bricks on wheelbarrows from where they had been heaped up. His cousin was married but did not live with his family. Handwell did the washing and the cooking. After working there for a month, he went to Tembo Village to start schooling.

Chapter 3: Handwell Goes back to School

Handwell found it difficult to start school again, although he had now enough money to buy clothes and pay school fees for at least two years. It was difficult to get a school transfer letter from Baula School in Mzimba. The nearest school to Tembo Village was Kawere, but he was not accepted there because the headmaster, Mr Chiusiwa, refused to enrol him without a transfer letter from the previous school. The other one was a Catholic full primary school at Mponela about 7 km from Tembo village. He was accepted there without a transfer letter after he had stated the reasons why it was difficult to go to Baula School in Mzimba and get the letter. He was enrolled in standard 7 on condition that, if he performed poorly, he would go back to standard 6. Handwell performed very well such that the following year he was promoted to standard 8. The equivalents were as follows: The then standard 3 was standard 5, standard 4 was standard 6, standard 5 was standard 7 and standard 6 was standard 8. So Handwell moved from standard 5 to standard 7.

He walked 14 km each day to and from school. He did not have breakfast or lunch during schooldays. On Saturdays and Sundays, he had lunch and supper only. If a meal was taken at ten or eleven o'clock in the morning, it was taken as lunch and the next meal would be supper as the last meal of the day no matter at what time it was taken.

In those days Handwell's faith in God grew stronger and stronger and he often experienced spiritual instructions from what he called the "disembodied" voice. He enrolled as a catechumen at Machenche CCAP and was later baptized in October 1963 by Rev J. Kamwana, the father of Rev Dr Jonathan Kamwana. He prayed regularly, even before reading and studying his books and notes. In 1964 he wrote standard 8 primary school leaving examinations. There were fifty-two pupils who wrote the examinations at

Mponela School and only two pupils passed, these were Davie Kabowa and Handwell Hara. Kabowa was selected to start form 1 at Dedza Secondary School, popularly known as Box 48. Handwell was selected as a pupil teacher that after teaching for a year he would go for a teacher training course if he passed the teacher training entrance examination.

Handwell knew very late that he was selected to teach as a pupil teacher. However, he thanked God that he was not selected to go to secondary school because he could not afford to pay school fees. After teaching as a pupil teacher at Nkhamanga School, he was called for a written teacher training entrance interview. He passed the examination and was posted to do his training at St John's Teacher Training College in Lilongwe in 1965-1967.

The teacher training course was for two years and it was the lowest grade that was being offered at that time. While he was doing the training, he also studied for the Junior Certificate Education. He passed the JC in 1968 after one year in teaching and he was promoted from T4 to T3 grade. Having passed the Junior Certificate, he continued studying for the Malawi School leaving examination by correspondence. He took English Language, Biology, English Economic History, Bible Knowledge and British Constitution. He passed these subjects at the level of General Certificate of Education with London University. He avoided the Cambridge and the Malawi school leaving examinations. The General Certification of Education (GCE) with London University was regarded as equivalent to Malawi School Certificate of Education (MSCE).

He began teaching in primary schools at the age of 25 years and he taught at different schools covering all classes from standard 1 to standard 8.

Now his call to the Holy Ministry to become an Evangelist and a Pastor grew stronger and stronger and he was not satisfied to remain a teacher. For several times he applied for pastoral training at Nkhoma Synod but all his applications were not successful. He applied to Livingstonia Synod and again his application was not successful. The reason that the Synods gave was that they did not know Handwell well. However, he was assured by the "disembodied" voice that he would be an evangelist and a pastor and that he would do his work in different areas, some of which he remembered when he became a pastor. He continued teaching and managed to help train his elder brother to be a driver—something he could not have done if he had gone for the pastoral training. He did part time preaching in the congregations he was attached to as a member.

Chapter 4: Handwell's Married Life and his Theological Training

Before Handwell passed Form Two Junior Certificate examination he married Lotasi Lungu, the daughter of Village Headman Samu (Chidothi) Lungu of Mponela in Dowa district in 1967. Handwell and Lotasi had a number of things of interest in common. Both were CCAP members from Machenche congregation. They both experienced dreams which turned to be true and straight forward. Handwell would be stopped from making a journey by a "disembodied" voice or stopped from doing things. The voice was followed by making Handwell feel reluc-

Lotasi Lungu

tant to continue the journey or doing something. He would sometimes feel tongue tied to continue whatever he was speaking and then completely change the subject. Lotasi had similar experiences. Both would know the death of someone before the actual death happened.

When Handwell dreamed of a person, who was seriously ill, and then was well and healthy, it meant that the person was dead. If he dreamed that a person has left his wife or her husband, then it meant that the person would leave his or her work. Often his dreams did not leave him wondering of their meanings. Handwell would tell from the look of things their end results and would shed tears before the results were actually out. He prayed several times to have such experiences removed from him, but they never stopped completely but became less frequent. When Dr W. Kawale was at the Bible Society, Handwell knew that he would become the General Secretary of Nkhoma Synod after a short time at the Bible Society. Handwell went to see Dr Kawale in his office at the Bible Society and told him that he would be the next General Secretary of Nkhoma Synod to succeed Rev A.A. Sasu. This came true and he was the General Secretary for six years.

Even though Handwell and Lotasi were Presbyterians, they would worship God in any other Christian Church and they harboured no hatred against people because of their beliefs. Handwell was a teacher in the Roman Catholic schools for ten years and was a lecturer at Zomba Theological College for more than twelve years where there were students from Presbyterian, Anglican, Baptist, Churches of Christ and Methodist denominations. Handwell and Lotasi lived with people of different races in the USA, in Scotland and in South Africa and they felt at home in all these places just

as they felt at home in Malawi in Zomba, Blantyre, Lilongwe, Dowa and Mzuzu. Handwell even felt that he could be able to stay alone without feeling lonely because of his experiences at the University of Pretoria where he was the only black man doing his studies. At first, he felt lonely and homesick, but later on he got used and lived happily alone.

Handwell and Lotasi did not have any biological children but their home was always full of children right from the time they got married. Handwell was told in a dream in the night that he had just married that he would not have children with her. He disregarded the dream through the influence of the relatives and he and the relatives tried hard to find support from both the biomedical field and traditional medicine but to no avail. In Grand Rapids Michigan the doctors at Blodgett Hospital were puzzled when they tried their best to help Lotasi have a child but failed. These experiences that Handwell and Lotasi went through strengthened their faith and helped them rely on God even more. They knew that God does not lie nor change his mind. Whatever he promises, he does; he speaks and it is done (Numbers 23:19). Lotasi was a wonderful woman for she knew people's secrets without being told—she was psychic. She was the person Handwell was most afraid of because he could not hide things from her.

After applying several times to the three Regional Synods, he was instructed by the voice to apply to Nkhoma Synod where it turned out that he would be trained as a pastor. When he applied again, he was accepted for training as a pastor in 1972 at the age of 30 years. So he resigned as a teacher for Lilongwe Diocese and joined Nkhoma Synod in 1972 and was posted to Chitalala Full Primary School. He did not teach at Chitalala because then he had to go to Nkhoma Theological College in Lilongwe. From 1963 the College trained pastors for all three regional Synods—Livingstonia, Nkhoma, Blantyre—and some students came from Harare Synod. The training lasted four years. Handwell joined the training in

1972 and graduated in 1975. There was a calling system of pastors in Nkhoma congregations for those who were already in ministry by transfer and for those who joined the ministry as their first appointment. In their last year of training, Nkhoma Synod students were advertised in *Kuunika* Magazine, with their pictures showing and stating that these were in their last year and therefore were eligible for calling for pastoral work.

After training in 1975 Handwell was left at the theological college for several months without getting any call while his classmate Rev Wesley Martin Kazemba, then unmarried, was called to several congregations—although traditionally Nkhoma Synod did not ordain an unmarried person for pastoral work. Since Kazemba was ordained first before Handwell, he went to attend his ordination and participated with a smile and wishing him well in the ministry.

Later on, Handwell was called by two congregations, namely Chileka and Mdika CCAP, in Lilongwe and Dowa respectively. He accepted the call from Chileka and was ordained in August 1975. Chileka CCAP is in T/A Kalolo with Namitete as a trading centre. At Chileka CCAP there is a Health Clinic, a trading centre, a primary school called Kalolo and a community Day Secondary School. Chileka CCAP had thirty-six zones or prayer houses and thousands of communicant members. While he was at Chileka CCAP from 1975 to 1978, he applied to several universities for further theological studies through Nkhoma Synod office since he had already passed GCE on ordinary level with the University of London. He was now doing A Levels with the same university. Rev Chris Human, a missionary from South Africa working in the Synod office as the Deputy General Secretary when the General Secretary was away for studies, processed Handwell's application in cooperation with Rev Olivier, the then Principal of Nkhoma College. Nkhoma College then had broken into two—Livingstonia and

Blantyre Synods went to Blantyre having Kapeni Teacher Training College turned into a Theological College.

In 1978 Nkhoma Theological College was short of tutors and the Synod asked Handwell to be a tutor there while his application to go to Calvin College and Seminary was being considered. So from October 1978 to May 1979 Handwell was a tutor at Nkhoma Theological College teaching Church History and Christian Ethics. This was a good preparation for his further theological studies at Calvin College and Seminary. He did very well in Church History and Ethics, so he was exempted from studying the two subjects. Instead, he studied Moral Philosophy and Philosophy of Religion. While he was a tutor at Nkhoma College he privately studied Greek and Hebrew; the Missionary tutors working at Nkhoma College were his private instructors. The knowledge of Greek and Hebrew helped him when he studied these languages in depth at Calvin College.

In May 1979 Handwell left Malawi for Calvin College and Seminary in Grand Rapids. He studied Classical Greek and Philosophy at the College for five months. It was an intensive course. He studied Hebrew at the Seminary for two months before he was enrolled for Masters in Theological Studies. Greek and Hebrew were much used in Biblical Studies and in Systematic Theology. In 1981 he graduated at Calvin Seminary with a Master of Theological Studies majoring in Systematic Theology. Before Handwell came back to Malawi Rev Dr Herman Kamnkhwani had finished his Bachelor of Divinity studies at the University of the North and was posted to

Zomba Theological College as a lecturer. When the Synod met in April, 1981 he was elected General Secretary, thus creating a vacancy at Zomba Theological College. So Handwell was called by the Synod to go to Zomba Theological College as a lecturer in the same year 1981 to replace Dr H. Kamnkhwani.

Chapter 5: Handwell as Lecturer, Pastor and Doctoral Student (1981-1988)

From 1981 to 1984 Handwell was a lecturer at Zomba Theological College. There were three Malawian lecturers—David Mphande, Aaron Kapenda and Handwell Hara representing Livingstonia, Blantyre and Nkhoma Synods respectively. Each of them had a Master's degree. This was the first time Zomba Theological College had three Malawians having Master's degrees as lecturers. Handwell became Dean of Student Affairs and Rev. Aaron Kapenda was the Principal. However, Rev D. Mphande left the college because he was not satisfied with the salaries and joined Blantyre Teacher Training College as a tutor. Handwell taught Systematic Theology, Christian Ethics, Philosophy of Religion and Church History for all the three years he was at Zomba Theological College. While still there he enrolled for Doctor of Divinity studies with the University of Pretoria in 1983.

In 1984 Handwell was called to Mdzobwe CCAP as a pastor. He continued his doctoral studies with the University of Pretoria. Mrs Mzandu, whose husband was the mayor of Lilongwe, offered to type his assignments because he did not know how to type, and the University required all assignments to be submitted in typed form. He visited the University several times to discuss his work with his promoters—Professors C.J. Wethmar and Dion Crafford.

While he was at Mdzobwe CCAP as a pastor and still a part time student of the University of Pretoria, he was elected Nkhoma Synod Clerk in 1985. This is one of the highest positions in the Synod. It is a position held by a person in the Synod Standing Committee (Moderamen). The Committee comprises the Moderator, Vice Moderator, Synod Clerk and Deputy Synod Clerk. The General Secretary is an ex-officio member at the Moderamen meetings, the Synodical meetings and at the Synod general meetings. He is the chief administrator of the Synod attending to the implementation of the Synod meetings' resolutions. The Synod Clerk is one of the Moderamen members involved in policy making matters. He is responsible for taking and correcting minutes of the Synod meetings through the recording clerks before handing them to the General Secretary to see the resolutions' implementation. He advises the General Secretary after his consultation with the Moderator when to call members for meetings.

From 1983 to 1987 Handwell struggled with his studies. He was sent many books to read and he did a lot of written assignments and tests. It was required that he should go and stay at the University to complete his studies because frequent consultations with his promoters were needed. He applied for a six months study leave from the Synod which was granted on condition that Mdzobwe CCAP would look after his family while he was away. In 1987 he left for the University and after passing several tests, his doctoral thesis proposal was approved and then he started working at it. At that time, University of Pretoria was only for white people and Handwell used the library for reading and writing. He consulted his promoters in their offices at the appointed times. He lived on the Campus in his own house with all facilities provided.

Handwell was granted study leave because he was called to Mdzobwe CCAP and in 1985 he was elected as Synod Clerk, a position that made him be a member of the Moderamen. This position made him visit the University often before he went there for six months to write his thesis. However, he applied to the Synod for an additional one month which was again granted.

He finished writing his doctoral thesis in 1988 and he graduated on 22 March 1989, becoming the first Doctor in Theology in Nkhoma Synod and the first black man to study and graduate at the University of Pretoria.[11] The Synod did not assign him to another work within the Synod but he returned to Mdzobwe CCAP as their pastor, and he maintained his position as the Synod Clerk. Later on, his position as the Synod Clerk was taken over by Rev Dr Jonathan Kamwana through casting votes and he became Deputy Synod Clerk. When the Synod wanted to remove him from being the Deputy Clerk by posting him from Mdzobwe CCAP to Namon Katengeza Church Lay Training Centre to be the Director, he refused because the centre's main work was not training the laity but holding conferences for different organizations. He felt that he would be busy with the centre's activities of buying food and the arrangements of the conferences and accommodation.

---

[11] The thesis was published as Handwell Yotamu Hara, *Reformed Soteriology and the Malawian Context*, Zomba: Kachere, 2008.

Chapter 6: Handwell as Education Secretary for Nkhoma Synod Schools

In 1992 Handwell was called by the Synod to be the Education Secretary for Nkhoma Synod schools to replace Rev Dr Winston Kawale who had left for Stellenbosch University for doctoral studies. From 1992-1996 Handwell was the Education Secretary. His main work was to maintain Christian discipline in all Nkhoma Synod schools by prioritizing Bible Knowledge and appointing Christian head teachers in these schools in consultation with the Ministry of Education. The Ministry would not allow to appoint a Christian head teacher who was not academically qualified for the position. Only people who had passed well Form IV and trained as T2 teachers were eligible to be appointed as heads for primary schools and those with a degree would be appointed heads for secondary schools.

In order to maintain Christian values and discipline in these schools it was resolved that the schools should be taken back to be completely under the Synod's control. The Synod had to build class-room blocks, pay teacher salaries and appoint head teachers. To do all these things, the Synod had to charge fees that would be enough to meet the expenses of running the schools. During this time the government had introduced free primary education and many parents preferred free to fee-paying primary education.

Handwell, backed by the Synod through the agency representatives and school committee chairpersons, discussed the possibility of taking back some schools to be under the Synod. The following primary schools were taken back during his term of office as Education Secretary: Dedza, Lilongwe and Chidothi at Mponela. The school committee chairpersons of these schools worked hard helping Handwell to take the schools back to the Synod. In Dedza the school committee chairperson was Mr

Chikakuda, in Lilongwe it was Mr Chithambo, and at Chidothi it was Mr Chimalizeni.

At the time of taking these schools back to the Synod, people were free to send their children either to free public primary schools or to paying primary schools. The Synod did not take back the schools which were not near a public school. The aim was that parents who would fail to pay fees for their children could send them to the nearby free public school. For instance, Madisi Full Primary School was not taken back because Mtanila Full Primary School had already more pupils than required and parents who could not pay fees would have been denied their children's education. The school at Kasungu Boma had been moved to a location where it was the only school and therefore it was not taken back to the Synod.

Handwell ran many Christian School Seminars to enlighten and educate teachers on the value of integrating Christian principles with core subjects such as Geography, History, Social Studies, Mathematics and Life Skills. Bible Knowledge was taken as the chief subject to help pupils aspire for wisdom with the motto "The fear of the Lord is the beginning of wisdom." Bibles and Nkhoma Synod catechism books were distributed in all schools. The schools were headed by Christian teachers. However non-Christians and Christian teachers of other denominations were also employed provided they were qualified and promised to abide by the rules and policies governing Nkhoma Synod Schools.

Taking back Nkhoma Synod secondary schools was more difficult than it had been with primary schools. It was because at the time the project started, there were three schools – Robert Blake in Dowa, William Murray in Lilongwe and Mlanda Girls in Ntcheu. The Synod did not participate much in the discussions of taking back some of these schools and Handwell would not do it as he did with the primary schools.

The first Girls' Christian Secondary school was built in Dowa at Mvera CCAP where there was the Lilongwe – Salima road construction camp. After finishing this road, the structures were given to the Synod and the site became Mvera Girls Christian Secondary School and Mr Makombe, who had just retired from the teaching service, was appointed its first head teacher. The advantage of appointing Mr Makombe as the head teacher was threefold; his house was within walking distance to the school; he had a degree in teaching from Chancellor College and was a CCAP Christian of Mvera congregation. Rev Dr K.J. Mgawi was very instrumental in negotiating with the in- charge of the Lilongwe – Salima road construction to have the camp site given to the Synod after the road construction was over. Electricity came to the camp and to the Mission station through the road constructors.

Handwell loved his work as the Education Secretary. He bought a maize mill for the department as an income generating activity and a vehicle to facilitate travel for the Education Secretary from his office to the schools. He employed many Christian teachers in the government unassisted schools with the intention to upgrade

the schools to full primary Christian schools like Dedza, Lilongwe and Chidothi. The Agency Representatives helped Handwell to run the schools and he provided them with new push bicycles for use in visiting and supervising the teachers.

Chapter 7: Handwell at ZTC, GMTI and Mzuzu University as a Lecturer

After Rev Dr Herman Kamnkhwani, who was the principal at Zomba Theological College, had died and Rev Dr W.E. Chikakuda had gone to Mozambique, Nkhoma Synod had no lecturers at Zomba, so Handwell was asked to go to Zomba in December 1996. Handwell did not want to go, but the Synod had no one then qualified to replace Dr Chikakuda. He accepted the Synod's request and went to Zomba. The principal was Rev Dr Dolb Mwakanandi representing Harare Synod. Dr Silas Nyirenda, Dr W. Manda and Dr Gordon represented Blantyre Synod; Dr Kang and Dr S. Chiphangwi represented Blantyre Synod and Handwell represented Nkhoma Synod. This was the first time when Zomba Theological College had been staffed by doctors in theology as lecturers.

Drs Mwakanandi, Kang, Gordon and Nyirenda started discussions with the Theology and Religious Studies Department of Chancellor College to introduce a BD programme at Zomba Theological College. Chancellor College asked ZTC to involve St Peter's Seminary in the discussions and this was agreed. However, Zomba at first went ahead with the BD programme preparations. Both Zomba and St Peters had qualified lecturers to teach in the BD program. ZTC began the programme but St Peter's started after it was officially accepted. Handwell was not much involved in the BD degree discussions but contributed in the formulation of the degree syllabus. He was also interested in the teaching. The Dean of Humanities and Dr Klaus Fiedler from Chancellor College played a big role to have the BD programme put in place and Dr Mwakanandi also did his best to meet with some people of influence such as the Vice Chancellor by inviting him to present Diploma papers at the graduation ceremonies.

Besides lecturing, Handwell was the Dean of Student Affairs from 1997 to 2006. He was relieved of this position when he was appointed the Vice Principal. His position as the Dean of Student Affairs gave him an experience of working with the students, the principal and members of the staff. Before the BD programme started Zomba Theological College had students from different denominations – the CCAP from Malawi, Zimbabwe and Zambia, the Anglican Council of Malawi and the Churches of Christ. Some students from the Methodist Church, the Roman Catholic and the Baptist Church came on their own when the degree began. Handwell continued lecturing in Systematic Theology, Theology of the Sacraments and Theology of Ecumenism. All BD students, by permission from their denominations, worshipped at the neighbouring Anglican Church, the Baptist Church and the Churches of Christ prayer house at Zomba Central Hospital.

Handwell and the BD students found the integration of ecumenical studies with the attending of prayers in different denominations very awarding. They appreciated the other students' faith rooted in their various denominational doctrines. This was a good preparation for Handwell's lecture work at Mzuzu University from 2009 to 2012. He also worked part time as a lecturer in Philosophy of Religion at Chancellor College and in Greek, Systematic Theology, and in Philosophy of Religion at Zambezi College of Ministry in Blantyre. As a lecturer at ZTC he also worked as a TEEM Director—a position which made him attend different theological conferences in many institutions in Africa. Some lecturers at ZTC were jealous of Handwell's position as the TEEM Director because with the allowances he received from TEEM office and because his popularity at ecumenical institutions outside Malawi made him outshine his ZTC colleagues.

Dr S. Nyirenda retired, followed by the Principal Dr Mwakanandi. Then Dr S. Chiphangwi, who was Vice Principal to Dr Mwakanandi, became the Principal. Rev S. Mazizwa was elected Deputy General

Secretary of Nkhoma Synod, while Rev Timothy Nyasulu was appointed Vice Principal. During all this time, Handwell continued his work as a lecturer and part time worker in various spheres.

Rev T. Nyasulu left for America for further studies and the Board appointed Handwell as the Vice Principal since they did not have anyone else to take this position and Handwell was now the only experienced lecturer at the institution. Even when they appointed Rev Mazizwa and Rev Nyasulu they might have felt guilty for over-looking Handwell, unless he was too unqualified for the position. However, Handwell fared well under those Vice Principals.

In 2007 Dr Chiphangwi intended to retire due to his frequent illnesses and physical weakness. When Dr Chiphangwi retired, Handwell, who was the Vice Principal, was not appointed the Principal, perhaps it was because he was not qualified for the position, or because of other reasons known to the Board itself. However, Handwell did not remain at the college but was made to retire together with Dr Chiphangwi. So both the Principal and the Vice Principal retired in the same month - 31st December, 2007. Dr Chiphangwi was given a congregation in Blantyre by his Synod and Handwell was appointed the Principal of Josophat Mwale Theological Institute (JMTI) by his Synod at Nkhoma.

Rev Anderson Muthambala was the Principal of Josophat Mwale and Rev Zeze was the Vice Principal. The transition of principalship from Muthambala to Handwell was not a good one. When Handwell was appointed the principal, he was not given accommodation because Muthambala had not yet been transferred from his house to another. So Rev Muthambala and Rev Zeze continued working as lecturers and principal and vice principal respectively while Handwell was waiting to be transferred to Nkhoma when the house would be available. This also created housing problem at ZTC because Handwell still occupied the house of ZTC. After three months of waiting, Handwell went to Nkhoma where the situation was not good. The handover of office work was poorly done since the ex-principal had retired as principal while Handwell was there as a mere lecturer giving him not any position. It was natural that Rev Muthambala behaved in the way he did as he became very uncooperative with Handwell. Handwell would not know well how Rev Muthambala solicited funds from the congregations and from outside donors for administration, lecturers' salaries, student allowances and for the wages of College workers. There was nothing wrong with Rev Muthambala carrying out the handover as he did, but there was something wrong with the Synod administrators. They did the same thing when Rev Katundu was appointed head teacher at Robert Blake Secondary School and the results were worse.

The relationship at JMTI among the staff members, among the students and between the students and the staff members was bad, lacking coordination and co-operation. Handwell found it hard to raise enough money for running the institution. His files were often missing from the office which made it difficult to find the right addresses of the donors inside Malawi and outside.

The joining of JMTI to other colleges for granting the status of awarding Diploma to theological students helped Handwell raise lecturers' salaries from the new incoming students' fees. The Board for Theological Studies would not allow that JMTI should be given the status of awarding Diploma in Theology if the annual intake of Diploma students was irregular. So Handwell, in consultation with the other lecturers, made the entrance to diploma studies open to all students who qualified, male or female.

However, the Board for JMTI had to endorse the proposal of awarding diplomas and opening the entrance to all who qualified but that they would not automatically become pastors after finishing their studies. The JMTI Board sent this request to the Moderamen and the Moderamen, after approval, sent the matter to the Synodical Committee which endorsed it as approved by the Synod. The JMTI lecturers did not complain of low salaries because of the allowances they received from Diploma students' fees. The Diploma students in the first year were few but later on the number increased.

In 2009 Handwell joined Mzuzu University as a lecturer in Systematic Theology and Philosophy of Religion where he worked for three years, 2009 to 2012. When he came back after his contract expired with Mzuzu University, Nkhoma Synod did not publish his name in the Church circular letter to show that he was available and legible for a call to the congregations, nor did the Synod assign him any work. He stayed at his residence at Msundwe from July to October 2012, then in November he joined the College for Christian Ministries (CCM) of the Anglican Church in Lilongwe.

In February 2013 an orphanage in Mchinji called Home of Hope appointed Handwell (now in his seventies) the Principal of its primary and secondary schools. He accepted the appointment although the salary was very low for the following reasons: he was a co-founder trustee and he had been a member and a secretary for the first 10 years of the existence of the orphanage. He felt that it was God's call to help Rev Thomson John Chipeta, who was now an elderly man in his 80s. The work of running the orphanage as a Director was in the hands of Lucy Malitowe Chipeta. The management team comprised of his grandchildren. Handwell's work was to supervise the teachers and see that teaching and learning went on well in order to prepare the children for a future independent life.

On 12 July, 2012 Handwell experienced an unusual change in his spiritual life that caused him to be fearless of any physical or spiritual danger around him. This event took place after his contract ended with Mzuzu University and it helped him not to complain of not being called by any congregation for the six months that he stayed at Msundwe Trading Centre. He re-organized his non-governmental organization which he had founded and registered in 2008 while he was at Justo Mwale Theological

Institute. He dismissed some old board members and replaced them with new members. The organization is called Christian Life-style Ministry whose work is to help the poorest of the poor in T/A Kalolo, Lilongwe.

The old Board members were:

- Dr Handwell Yotamu Hara — Chairperson
- Mrs Banda (Masintha CCAP) — Vice Chairperson
- Mr Charles Kapitapita — Secretary
- Rev David Kawanga — Vice Secretary
- Rev Joseph H. Chimutu — Treasurer
- Mrs Lotasi Hara — Board member
- Mrs Enala Khombe — Board member

The new members were:

- Mr Austin Chidzenje replacing Mrs Banda
- Mr Nelson Muganda replacing Rev Davis Kawanga
- Mr Simoko replacing Rev Joseph H. Chimutu
- Mrs Mugada replacing Mrs Enala Khombe

The board of the re-organized Christian Lifestyle Ministry (CLM) met frequently because these new members were all from Msundwe Trading Centre. The work which had stopped for some time resumed and a number of the poorest people were helped with new and used clothes, used pairs of shoes from both Board members and well-wishers. Some of the people during December 2012 and February 2013 had their houses thatched with plastic papers and grass. Food was given to those that lacked and two schools had their third term fees paid by CLM.

Handwell continued living at Msundwe Trading Centre and doing part time lecturing at CCM in Lilongwe. He was instructed by the "disembodied" voice that the first pay he received from CCM should be spent on buying the necessities for the poorest of the poor and he obeyed the advice after telling it to Lotasi who encouraged him to do as he was told. He instituted a local committee whose work was to find out the poorest of the poor to be helped within Msundwe Trading Centre at T/A Kalolo, South East community. Among the poorest of the poor, there were three blind women and one blind man. Another one was a man who had had a stroke and struggled moving from one place to another. Another person had a withered leg and walked with the support of a stick. There were those who were poor due to old age and to negligence by their relatives. How long Handwell will run that organization and continue to be the Principal of Hope Schools, only God knows. I wish him God's blessings as he ministers for the Lord.

POSTSCRIPT

By Rev Dr Winston Kawale

Prof Klaus Fiedler asked me to write this postscript. To him the reason was that Dr Hara and myself worked together at Mzuzu University. But to me it was more than that. We both were ministers in Nkhoma Synod. Furthermore, although Dr Hara was a senior minister to me, we developed a lasting friendship. He started it. When I was at Mlanda Congregation, Dr Hara came all the way from Zomba Theological College where he was teaching. He came to ask me to apply for further theological studies in the USA. This gave me a desire to go further studies. I did not go to that seminary but instead went to St Paul's University in Kenya. Later when I was the Coordinator of Chichewa Study Bible at the Bible Society of Malawi in Blantyre, again Dr Hara came all the way from Zomba Theological College to see me. When he entered my office he said "I am here as an Angel from the Lord. I have this message to tell you. At the forthcoming Nkhoma Synod Assembly you will be elected General Secretary." Dr Hara has narrated this in this book. I thought it was a joke. No! It wasn't, it happened. I was elected General Secretary at the very first voting. It was due to this relationship that while I was at Mzuzu University, there was an advert for a lecturer for Systematic Theology. I called and asked Dr Hara if he could apply. He did, and we were together lecturing at Mzuzu University.

The Rev Dr Handwell Hara died on 13 July 2018 and was laid to rest on 16 July 2018 at the Heroes Acre of Mchinji Home of Hope. The funeral was attended by many people which included large numbers of clergy from different denominations. Some of these ministers were Dr Hara's former students at Zomba Theological College and Josophat Mwale Theological Institute. There were many Church leaders. In his eulogy, the General Secretary of

Nkhoma Synod, Rev V. Kachipapa, gave a detailed life history of Dr Hara, starting with the day of birth on 9 February 1942, his baptismal date on 24 October 1963, date of his starting theological training in 1972, his attaining Bachelor of Theology at the University of London; Master of Theology at Calvin Theological Seminary; and Doctor of Divinity at the University of Pretoria. Rev Kachipapa also narrated various responsibilities Dr Hara held in Nkhoma Synod, at Zomba Theological College, at Josophat Mwale Theological Institute and at Mzuzu University.

The Nkhoma Synod Moderator, Rev Nkhoma, gave a moving testimony of Dr Hara's humility wherever he served. Other speakers included the Principal of Zomba Theological College who revealed to the gathering that Dr Hara was the first black African to take a doctorate degree at the University of Pretoria during the apartheid era in South Africa. He told the gathering that the University of Pretoria was, at the death of Dr Hara, arranging to honour him for being the first black African student. He said that upon hearing of the death of Dr Hara, the University of Pretoria authorities said that the arrangement to honour Dr Hara would still be done.

Other dignitaries at the funeral included Rev Dr T. Nyasulu , the Moderator of the CCAP General Synod; Bishop Magangani of the Anglican Diocese of Northern Malawi; Rev Dr L. Nyondo, General Secretary of Synod of Livingstonia; and Bishop G. Matonga, the General Secretary of Malawi Council of Churches.

Rev M. Kadawati preached a very moving sermon and Rev Dr W. Kawale presided over the committal service at the grave.

Upon visiting Rev Chipeta, the Founding Director of Mchinji Home of Hope, for more information on Dr Hara, Rev Chipeta said that he shared about the founding of Home of Hope to Dr Hara in 1996. Dr Hara agreed and later became a Board of Trustees member. When Dr Hara retired in 2012, the Management of Home of Hoped asked him to join the management there as Director of

Education. During his service at the Home of Hope, Dr Hara and Rev Chipeta negotiated with the Ministry of Education and a Memorandum of Understanding was signed in which the Ministry was able to send teachers to the school of Home of Hope. They also negotiated with the Ministry of Labour for them to provide training at the Vocational Training Centre of the Home of Hope.

Rev Chipeta also showed me a WILL in which they stated that the two of them, upon their death, would be buried at the Mchinji Home of Hope Heroes Acre. It also states that when they will die, their wives will be kept and cared for by the Home of Hope till their death and will also be buried at the Heroes Acre.